✶TRACEY✶

THEME PARK
DESIGNER

The Look Up Series #5

TRACEY

THEME PARK DESIGNER

Real Women in S.T.E.A.M.

Aubre Andrus

ADJECTIVE
ANIMAL
PUBLISHING

Look UP
SERIES

"FOR THE GIRLS WHO ALWAYS DREAM ABOUT WHAT THEY'LL BE ONE DAY." — AA

Published by Adjective Animal Publishing in Santa Monica, California.

Visit us online at adjectiveanimalpublishing.com.

Design: Alice Connew
Photography: Ariel Moore
Logos: Shay Merritté
Illustrations: Aubre Andrus

6, Cat illustration: Tracey Noce; 6, 58, Paper clip illustration: Designed by rawpixel.com/ Freepik; 6, 58, Polaroid: Roland Deason/Unsplash; 8, Polaroid: Rochelle Lee/Unsplash; 8, Merry-Go-Round: Ethan Hoover/Unsplash; 8, Roller coaster: Ian Romie Ona/Unsplash; 11, Roller coaster: Mitchell Luo/Unsplash; 12, Theme park ride: Jason Chen/Unsplash; 18, Roller coaster: Priscilla du Preez/Unsplash; 18, Theme park: Jiongda Xu/Unsplash; 19, 51, Ride illustration: Tracey Noce; 23, Paper model construction photos: Adam Noce; 29, Jack rabbit: Don Biresch/Flickr; 35, Pelvis illustration: Tracey Noce; 36, Artist's studio: Laura Adai/Unsplash; 36, ArtCenter: Jchobanana/Flickr; 40, 42, 43, 58, Sketchbook interiors: Tracey Noce; 46, 58, Paintings: Tracey Noce; 55, Cat skeleton illustrations: Rush Shippen Huidekoper/Wikimedia; 56, Cat illustrations: Tracey Noce; 58, Leg illustration: Tracey Noce.

Library of Congress Cataloging-in-Publication Data is available upon request.

ISBN 9781639460205 (paperback)
ISBN 9781639460212 (hardcover)
ISBN 9781639460229 (e-book)

TABLE OF CONTENTS

CHAPTER 1
MEET TRACEY

Here's a drawing
of Simple Phil, one
of my three cats.

✍ DREAM IT, DRAW IT ✍

Look around you. Everything you see appeared in someone's imagination first. The chair. The water bottle. Your shoes. Even the way the letters look in this book. Someone had to draw it, design it, and then make it!

I'm Tracey, and I'm a theme park designer. I help create the experiences you find at theme parks like rides, parades, and themed lands. Everything you see in a theme park also **STARTED IN SOMEONE'S IMAGINATION.** An artist like me has to draw it, sculpt it, or paint it. Then we share it with a team of people who can turn our artwork into reality.

Drawing is a way to communicate with each other, just like talking or writing. Artists create images that make you think or feel something. Art can be anything—a sculpture in a museum, a map of a city, or a finger painting made by a toddler.

Some people think art is silly or unimportant. But artists are **highly-trained** people who use many skills to bring imagination and stories to life. It's not magic, it's hard work.

I might have a cool idea for a ride, but it takes a lot of people to bring that idea to life. Building a MAKE-BELIEVE WORLD in real life is complicated! We run into a lot of problems along the way. I work closely with engineers to solve these problems.

Theme park engineers make sure the rides we dream up are safe, strong, and move smoothly. They also make sure that all the mechanics, or moving parts that power the ride, fit inside the **ride vehicles** or spaces that we design.

For example, let's say I'm designing an underwater world. I want everything to **LOOK AWESOME AT ALL TIMES.** But in a theme park, people can walk around almost anywhere and I never know where their eyes are going to dart next.

In order to make a robotic octopus move the way we want it to, an engineer may need a big mechanical box. I don't want visitors to see the box, so I might hide it behind a rock or seaweed. I'd make sure that area has fewer details or a repeating pattern that doesn't draw too much attention. I also might arrange bright colors and main characters in a different area so the rider focuses on that instead.

It's a good thing I love solving problems like this! If the engineers and I do our jobs right, you'll never see things like power sources, lighting fixtures, wires, and safety systems. You'll just feel like **you're really transported** to another world!

SEEING SCIENCE

At any given time, humans can only focus on a quarter-sized space at once. That's why our eyes dart around so much. It's called **foveal vision**. Your brain processes these different images very quickly and stitches them together to create a larger view of what's around you. I consider this as I'm designing, and use design concepts like color, contrast, light, and shapes to catch someone's attention.

ℓ WHAT IS DESIGN? ℓ

Design isn't just about making pretty things—those things have to be useful, too. It might take a little bit of science, technology, art, and problem-solving in order to make a great design. **Design is where art meets function.** Function is how something is used or how it works.

Buildings are designed so they can stand on their own and people can live inside them. Cars are designed so people can drive long distances safely inside them. Lamps are designed to be turned on easily and light up a room.

Theme parks are designed so people can get on rides safely and quickly, and so they can HAVE FUN. But as a theme park designer, the experiences I create need to function for everyone. I have to be aware of how all different kinds of people experience a theme park.

Sometimes I visit a theme park, but I imagine I'm someone else, such as a deaf or hard of hearing person. I observe all the experiences as if I can't hear anything. I focus on smells and touch, and try to read all of the signs.

The next time I design a ride, I have a much better idea of how someone different than me might experience a theme park. **GREAT DESIGNS SHOULD WORK FOR EVERYONE.**

As much as I love dreaming, I don't design anything that can't be built in real life. If I am designing a roller coaster in a mountain, I know the mountain has to be less than 200 feet tall. Otherwise it needs a flashing light on top to alert airplanes! And that's probably not going to fit well in the imaginary world we are creating.

I also consider how many people can get on the ride at one time, and how many people can get on the ride per hour. In order to keep theme park visitors happy, rides need to keep people **moving on and off**—otherwise the lines would get too long.

When theme park designers are dreaming up thrill rides we also have to think about how fast the ride is moving and whether it might make people sick. We work with scientists who measure bodies in motion and can tell us whether or not they think our ride will make someone vomit. We jokingly call them **VOMITOLOGISTS!**

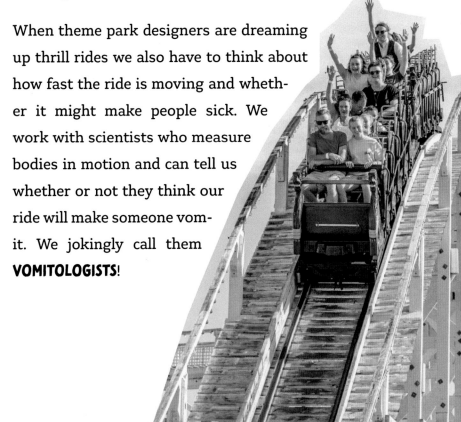

We also consider the lighting in a thrill ride. If you're moving really fast and the lights are flickering, some people can get very sick or uncomfortable. Special instruments can be used to check that the lighting is safe for everyone.

As you can see, there's a lot of math, science, and technology behind the art. Even though I'm very creative and artistic, I'm also very interested in the science of how things work. Being curious about the world around me has helped me become a better artist, a better designer, and a more well-rounded person.

Designers often need to know a little bit about everything in order to do their jobs well. Sometimes, identifying what you **don't know** is just as important as what you **do know**. That's why we work together as a team. Everyone is an expert on a different subject.

I love walking around theme parks and watching how people react when they're waiting in line and after they get off a ride that I designed. As an artist, **I'M ALWAYS OBSERVING**—which means carefully watching—the world around me.

At the end of the day, it's most important how I make someone feel. Theme parks use sight, sound, and smell to create an experience that people remember. People often visit theme parks with friends, family, and grandparents. Some of their most TREASURED MEMORIES might happen on a theme park ride that I designed.

I want these happy memories to stay with someone forever. It's kind of **like a gift I can give to strangers.** There are no credits at the end of a theme park ride like there are with a movie. Theme park visitors will never know that I created a ride. But I love knowing that my art will live on for years to come, and will continue to help people create special memories.

This is me! Who would have thought that one day I'd grow up to design rides?

ALL ABOUT TRACEY

I'm from...
Lake Havasu, Arizona

But now I live in...
Los Angeles, CA

Birthday:
October 18

Siblings:
I have three sisters
and two brothers!

TRACEY'S FAVORITES

Food:
Chicken Tikka Masala

Place:
Singapore

Ice Cream Flavor:
Mint Chip

Color:
Orange

Sport:
Gymnastics

**Ocean or
mountains?**
Mountains

**TV or
movies?**
TV

**Summer
or winter?**
Winter

**Chocolate
or vanilla?**
Chocolate

Pets:

I have three cats: Simple Phil (who is hearing impaired), Marbles, and Mote. I also have two desert tortoises, Petunia and Pansy.

What is something someone might not know about you?

I had a very rare kind of cancer, but I beat it! Because I like medical facts, it was interesting for me to learn all about it. Now I like to help others who have this kind of rare cancer better understand it.

What is something you wished you knew how to do?

I love plants, but I can't grow them! They always die. Instead, I like to identify them in nature and sketch them in my notebook. I also like to find native plants in my backyard that I can pick and feed to Petunia and Pansy.

What is your favorite hobby?

I love video games, especially open-world games. They are similar to theme-park design in that you can walk around everywhere and explore. You can't control where a player—or a theme park visitor—will go, so you have to make the whole world interesting and awesome.

CHAPTER 2
HOW THEME PARK RIDES GET MADE

✒ THE BIG IDEA ✒

Every new project starts with a small group of people. We gather in a room and brainstorm, which means we share ideas and dream big. We imagine what a **FUN RIDE** might be. We ask ourselves questions like:

- What kind of ride is this: a dark ride? Roller coaster? Water ride?

- Who is the ride for: little kids? Families? Thrill seekers?

- In what time period does this ride take place? And where?

- What kind of vehicle moves the riders around?

- What happens in the ride? What's the story?

- How should people feel? Scared or happy? Will this ride make them laugh?

I start with pencil and paper. I sketch what this idea might look like after the brainstorm. I try to draw a moment that perfectly captures the adventure. This is called CONCEPT ART. I want someone to look at the artwork and say, "Oh I get it! It's an underwater ride!"

As we're fine-tuning our idea, we'll ask others to join us. I'm a creative person who is focused on the story, but many expert team members can help us narrow down the details:

- A ride engineer can imagine how fast or slow a vehicle needs to go.

- A mechanical engineer could tell us how a robotic figurine will move.

- An industrial engineer will let us know how much space we need in order to fit a certain number of people.

- An architect can tell us how many columns are in the building so we can figure out our ride path.

Once we have a general sense of the story, how things look, and how the ride works, we will **pitch the idea**. In this case, pitching doesn't mean throwing a ball. A pitch is a meeting where we present the idea to our bosses, and they decide whether or not they think we should build the idea in real life. Building a ride is expensive, so we can't just make every idea we dream up.

My art is very important during this meeting. I may share paper artwork, a clay sculpture, or a virtual reality computer program. With just a few images, I need to convince people that **THIS IDEA IS AWESOME**. They need to quickly understand the story and how the ride might work. It feels great when I find out our idea will get made!

This is what a sketch looks like when I start thinking through a ride idea. This isn't shaded or colored yet.

✎ THE LITTLE DETAILS ✎

Once our idea is approved, it's time to figure out exactly where everything goes, how big it is, and what supplies we need to build it. We need to nail down exactly what every detail looks like, how long each scene in the ride might last, and what any characters might say. **Every sound, sight, and smell matters!**

Architects, engineers, and designers make a 3D model on the computer. Then we all work together to make decisions

Here's my desk at home. I draw on this big tablet with a digital pen.

like where to add wiring and pipes and where to place electrical equipment. I might have to change my design slightly. We don't want a pretty scene with air conditioning pipes running through the middle of it!

One time I wanted to design a ride vehicle that looked like a sleigh— long and rectangular. But for safety reasons, the engineers said the ride vehicle had to be a square shape. The engineer and I had to get creative and figure out how we could make a square shape look like a rectangular sleigh.

Engineers and artists think very differently. But that means we can come up with **INTERESTING SOLUTIONS** when we work together. On this particular problem, we passed some drawings back and forth until we finally came up with an idea—we'd make an optical illusion, which means we'd trick people's eyes into seeing something that wasn't really there.

By bending in the front corners and adding a deep scoop in the front, we made the square look more like a sleigh by ADDING CURVES. In the end, we were both happy with the design. My goal is always to make sure the story stays on track despite any changes that we might have to make along the way. The finished ride vehicle wasn't exactly like my original drawing, but it was close!

My designs will always be changed a little bit–there's no way I could predict every possible problem ahead of time! But one way that I can better plan ahead is by making models. As I build a model, I may figure out how to design something in a better way. It's helpful when I can see and touch something—even if it's miniature-sized.

TYPES OF THEME PARK RIDES

ROLLER COASTERS

Coasters dip, curve, and drop. Some even go upside down—that's called an inversion.

WATER RIDES

Riders float on a raft or boat with many people or plunge down a drop while riding a log.

DARK RIDES

Small vehicles take riders through a series of dark rooms that are themed with sets, robotic characters, and music.

MOTION SIMULATOR RIDES

The ride vehicle tilts up and down and side to side to match a video screen. It makes riders feel like they're really moving through a space.

TRANSPORTATION RIDES

Some rides, like trains and gondolas, have a second purpose—to move people from one side of the park to the other.

3D RIDES

Riders wear 3D glasses, which make a movie look three-dimensional instead of flat, while moving in a vehicle or sitting in a theater.

Models can be made from clay, paper, or foam. One of my favorite materials to use for model-making is a block or a sheet of yellow foam. It's lightweight and sturdy, and can easily be carved or cut with a sharp knife. That means I can add a lot of detail. Not only do these models help me solve problems, but they also help me sell my idea to other people. I want everyone to easily understand and love my idea.

Here I am turning a 2D drawing of a building into a 3D model.

This is a paper model. I'm folding and cutting some tiles for the roof.

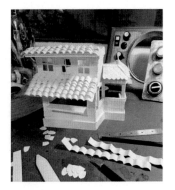

Now I have a better idea of how this design will look in real life.

Once we have our final designs approved by the architects and engineers, it's time for construction. I get to visit the theme park and watch the construction crews as they build. I'll let them know if something doesn't look right, and I might even pick up a paint brush or power tool to help them fix it. I'll grind down rocks, move a figurine, or touch up the paint in the background.

As much as I love brainstorming ideas, figuring out how to **turn that idea into reality** is the best part of being a theme park designer. I love solving problems with a huge group of very smart people. As we work through challenges, I learn a lot. I ask a lot of questions about subjects I don't know about. But I also get the chance to teach others.

I have drawers full of ideas that were never approved. Part of my job is to pitch ideas, and not all of those ideas get made. It's just the way it is! So when I see an idea of mine finally get built, it's REALLY MAGICAL. When the ride finally opens for the first time and I see people smiling, it's the coolest feeling—especially after four years of hard work and waiting!

WHO ELSE WORKS ON THEME PARK RIDES?

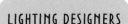

SOUND ENGINEERS are in charge of sound effects and speakers.

LIGHTING DESIGNERS decide how dim or bright a space will be, and can dream up cool projections and special effects with lights.

A COMPOSER creates a musical soundtrack for the ride.

WRITERS decide what characters will say in the ride.

ESTIMATORS figure out how much materials and construction might cost.

PRODUCERS keep everyone on schedule and find experts to work on the project.

PROJECT MANAGERS keep track of the construction crew's schedule and progress.

FROM IDEA TO THEME PARK RIDE

1. A theme park designer organizes a brainstorm, which is a meeting where people share cool ideas. No idea is a bad idea!

2. The designer takes one ride idea that stands out the most and imagines the story, what it looks like, and how it makes riders feel.

3. Engineers help decide how the ride will move, how big it will be, and how many people can ride it.

4. The designer creates concept art, which illustrates a scene from the ride and quickly shows a snapshot of what the adventure might look and feel like.

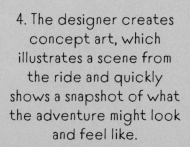

7. Lighting designers, sound engineers, and writers also add finishing touches to the ride.

8. Construction begins! The designer oversees the project and makes sure the story is clearly being told through every detail.

6. If the ride is approved, the designer creates a 3D model of their art. Engineers and architects finalize details like where wiring, pipes, and electrical equipment should go.

9. The ride is tested for safety, speed, and comfort.

5. The designer pitches the ride idea in a meeting and shares their artwork. The ride gets approved or rejected.

10. The ride opens! We love seeing visitors enjoy the ride for the first time.

CHAPTER 3
HOW DID I GET HERE?

✒ SCHOOL DAYS ✒

I grew up in a very small place in the middle of the California desert. It was a two hour bus ride to get to school. The closest city was in Arizona. Imagine spending four hours a day on a bus! I had to have a BIG IMAGINATION to keep myself entertained.

My curiosity kept me busy at home, too. I loved exploring the desert around our house and learning about plants, animals, and bugs. I **carried a journal** with me like I was an

adventurer. I would write notes in it and draw things that I observed, like rock carvings. I liked to create stories around the things that I saw.

For example, there were a lot of jackrabbits in the desert. I imagined they had very sophisticated underground villages. When I grew up, I learned that jackrabbits aren't even rabbits—they are hares. That means they don't burrow underground. Science has always interested me!

From age five, I **really struggled** with math and spelling. My mom always had to help me. We practiced spelling words and multiplication tables over and over again until I had them memorized. But I was a really good student in every other subject.

As I grew older, I continued to do really well in every subject except math. I had tutors, stayed after school, and even took summer school. I just couldn't get the hang of math. To me, it was impossible. Numbers were always a problem.

I had trouble counting things and counting spare change. I couldn't read the hands of a clock correctly until I was sixteen. I wasn't a good dancer because I had problems with repetition, patterns, and keeping to the beat. If someone gave me their phone number, it would take me three or four times before I wrote it down correctly. I even struggled with telling left from right!

Finally, in high school, my math teacher noticed that I did really well in every class but math. She brought in a specialist who, based on all my struggles with numbers, figured out that **I HAD DYSCALCULIA**. It's a learning difference that means I have difficulty making sense of numbers. I was so glad to finally learn what was going on in my brain.

I focused on how creative and artistic my brain was. I started solving math problems in a more creative way. I call it "artist's math." It's easier for me to use comparisons.

For example, I can use a six-foot-tall person as a form of measurement. If I want to know how tall a building is, I can imagine a bunch of six-foot-tall people stacked on top of each other to estimate how tall the building is. It's just easier for me to imagine something visually.

My creativity helped me become a better student in more ways than one. When I doodled in class, I remembered what the teacher was saying better. I later learned that brains process motor memories (like drawing) and language (like a teacher talking) differently. That's why I could draw and listen at the same time. How our brains work is something that has always fascinated me.

Many people think art is just a hobby or think they aren't good enough, so they stop. But I never lost **THAT LOVE OF DRAWING.** There's a reason why all little kids are interested in art—it's how we humans express ourselves!

LOTS TO LEARN

There are so many different kinds of learners like auditory (hearing), tactile (touch), and visual (seeing). How do you learn best? By listening to the teacher talk (auditory), by reading words in a book or seeing pictures (visual), or by experiencing and actively doing something yourself (tactile)?

When I was fifteen, my mom signed me up for an art class. I had never taken an art class before. It was a **figure drawing class**, which meant a model stood in the middle of the room and we had to draw their face and body.

The teacher gave me a lot of instructions. I had to learn how big certain parts of the human body should be and where certain muscles are located. I kept at it and IMPROVED, and the teacher eventually encouraged me to apply to art school.

Here I am painting in my childhood bedroom.

I had always dreamed of going to medical school to become a doctor. I was so interested in how our brains and bodies worked. But math really stressed me out, and I'd have to take a lot of math tests to get into medical school. This art class showed me how much science was behind art. I had learned so much about the human body already! Maybe I was actually meant to be an artist.

✐ OFF TO ART SCHOOL ✐

I worked on my portfolio throughout my senior year of high school. A portfolio is made up of about twenty-five pages of art that **showcase an artist's talents**. I submitted my portfolio to ArtCenter College of Design in Pasadena, California.

I was nervous. It was a really good school, and not a typical college. I had heard that ArtCenter was like medical school... **BUT WITH PAINT BRUSHES!** I was so excited when I learned that I was accepted! I was thrilled, but I knew that there was a lot of hard work ahead of me.

Art school was filled with all different kinds of creative people. Some students were photographers. Others wanted to design cars or make movies. I decided to major in entertainment design. I wanted to learn how illustrations could be used in theme parks, movies, video games, and more.

TRACEY'S UNIVERSITY

School: ArtCenter College of Design

Location: Pasadena, California

Major: Entertainment Design

This is ArtCenter's South Campus building. Can you spot the graffiti mural at the top?

FUN FACT!

Most of the teachers at ArtCenter College of Design are people who work in the design field and teach classes in their free time. They could be film directors, artists, or architects. They love their jobs so much that they want to share their knowledge with students. That's very different from a typical university that has professors, which are people whose only job is to teach.

Often art schools have studios where students can create their work. What would be in your art studio?

In art school, students take more than just painting and drawing classes. We still had to take math, science, history, and English classes. But all those classes were **tailored to art and design**. For example, in my English class, I learned how to write stories and characters for movies and TV shows. —

In my science class, we learned all about the science of eyeballs and how human brains take in information. That's where I learned about foveal vision, and how humans only focus on a quarter-sized space at a time.

We even dissected a human body and looked at all the muscles. Then we had to **BUILD A SKELETON** so we could memorize which bones belonged where. Knowing how every bone and muscle works helped me draw a human body even better. Artists have been

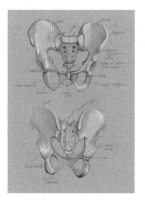

Here is just one of the drawings I've made of the human skeleton.

doing this for centuries. Did you know that Leonardo da Vinci used to sneak into graveyards to study human bodies?

My history classes were all about art, too. Artists and designers must know art history backward and forward—from the very first cave paintings to today. It helps me create themed rides and lands that feel real and are true to the time period.

I took a class on the **psychology of color**, which is a study of how color affects our moods and behaviors. For example, blue has been scientifically proven to be a very calming color. Red has the opposite effect on your brain and can even increase your blood pressure. That's probably why stop signs are red—red gets your attention!

I also enjoyed my cultural studies classes, where I learned about how people live around the world, and my design class, where I learned how to design things, like chairs, in the most comfortable way based on the human body.

By the end of art school, I had improved my drawing and painting skills and I had learned a ton of REALLY COOL information about how an image or an object could share a message with the world. I knew a little bit about a lot of things. But I wasn't sure what I wanted to do with it all!

My portfolio, which was now filled with drawings and paintings that could help me get a job, looked different from the other students' portfolios. It was a mix of make-believe maps and weird contraptions.

Someone at a theme park company liked my portfolio. I really didn't know what it meant to be a theme park designer. But I went to the job interview to learn more. They liked that I explained how things worked with my drawings. They saw that even though I was an artist, I was engineering-minded. Before I knew it, I had a job as a theme park designer!

I had a lot to learn at first. I was surrounded by people who knew **a lot more** than me. So, I asked a lot of questions and tried to learn very quickly. I made sure to explain my thought process to people, so they could understand how my brain works. Then, they'd tell me how they were thinking about something. Eventually, things got easier and I started to really understand theme park design.

Theme park designer ended up being the perfect job for me! I went on to create rides, themed lands, and experiences around the world. Being a curious kid—and now a curious adult—helps me every day at work. **NEVER STOP LEARNING!**

WHAT IS ART SCHOOL?

Tracey has a degree in entertainment design. Here's what that means and why she earned it.

Tracey went to art school for four years after high school. In order to go to art school, you must apply and get accepted. The most important part of your application is your portfolio, which features your best artwork, photographs, or film (depending on what type of art you'd like to specialize in).

People go to college to learn more about a specific career like entertainment design. After four years, if you've passed all of your classes, you get an undergraduate degree like Tracey did. It's a certificate that proves that you know a lot about a certain subject. Knowing a lot about a certain subject can help you find a good job.

WHAT IS A JOB?

Tracey's job is 'theme park designer.' Why do people like Tracey have a job?

People work at a job in order to make money, which can be used to pay for a place to live, food, clothing, and fun things like travel and entertainment. Jobs give people a sense of purpose, or a reason to use their talents every day. Jobs can also make the world a better place by helping other people or by solving big problems. You can meet cool people and learn new things at a job. Or even travel the world!

Have you ever made money by doing a chore or task?

What are some careers that you can think of?

What kind of jobs do the people in your life have?

Here I am sketching statues in a museum.

CHAPTER 4
DESIGN AROUND THE WORLD

NOTEBOOK

ℓ STORY TIME ℐ

When I design a theme park ride, land, or parade, I'm telling a story. As designers, we tell a lot of the story through images and objects. For instance, if we're creating a magical forest ride, we need to make people feel like they're really moving through lush trees and a grassy floor.

Theme park designers don't just go to the store and buy things—we often make them ourselves. If we need rocks, we'll build our own by covering a metal wire frame with mortar. Not only do they look real, but they'll be the exact size and shape we want.

My fake rock needs time to dry.

In order to make our storytelling realistic, we TRAVEL around the world a lot. I'm always making observations and getting what we call a 'sense of place.' Sure, you can look up some pictures on the internet. But going to the real place and **experiencing the sights, sounds, and smells in person** can't be beat. During a work field trip, I look at everything—from the tile on the floor to the sap on the tree to the color of the sky.

For example, one time I was designing a ride for a theme

park in another country. After visiting, I learned that the sky was often gray and overcast—not bright blue and clear like it is here in California. That detail helped me decide which colors I should choose for the building.

I have so many photos of random things like cracks in a wall, arrangements of rocks, and close-ups of paint colors that help make my work **LOOK MORE REAL**. We sometimes meet up with archaeologists, who are scientists that study historical objects and sites, to help us learn more about a place.

I always **bring my sketchbook** and draw what I see—just like I did when I was a kid! My sketchbook is filled with random drawings—a cool lamp I saw in Bali, an interesting window from New York City, and ancient Mayan ruins from Mexico.

I believe that sketching something is even better than taking a photo. Only after I sketch something do I really

Here are some pages from my sketchbook when I visited Mexico.

understand it. It helps me imagine what the designers or architects were thinking when they made this object.

I feel so lucky to have gone on these trips and to have learned about history, different cultures, and art. Some of these research trips have helped me **design things for my own house,** including a rock project in my backyard. When I'm done, they will look like real rocks, and will nicely cover up some pipes in my backyard.

Every day as a theme park designer is different. Sometimes, I'm wearing a construction hat and applying fifty pounds of glitter to a theme park ride very early before the park opens. Other times, I'm sketching Mayan ruins in Mexico on a research trip then turning one of my drawings into a clay sculpture back at work. I'm so thankful that my artistic skills and my curiosity led me here!

TRACEY'S ADVICE FOR YOUNG DESIGNERS

BE CURIOUS.

Pick something and learn everything you can about it. Take stuff apart. Learn how it works. Discover new things. It will make you a smarter, more well-rounded person. The more you know, the more you can express yourself.

OBSERVE THE WORLD.

Carry a journal with you and draw the things you see and like—plants, bugs, buildings, clouds, chairs, anything! When traveling to a new place, pay attention to why things look the way they do and how they are different.

DON'T LET OTHER PEOPLE STOP YOU.

Don't let other people squash your dreams. If you love bugs and want to be a bug scientist—do it! When I was younger, people thought only boys should be interested in the kinds of things I liked. I'm glad I didn't care what they thought.

IT'S OK TO FEEL UNCOMFORTABLE.

When you're just starting out, you have a lot to learn. Don't be afraid to ask questions. Learn from the people around you. They will help you grow.

ART IS A REAL CAREER.

We don't often think about the artists and designers who created all the things that surround us. But everything we come in contact with came from an artist's mind. Don't let anyone tell you, "No, you can't be an artist."

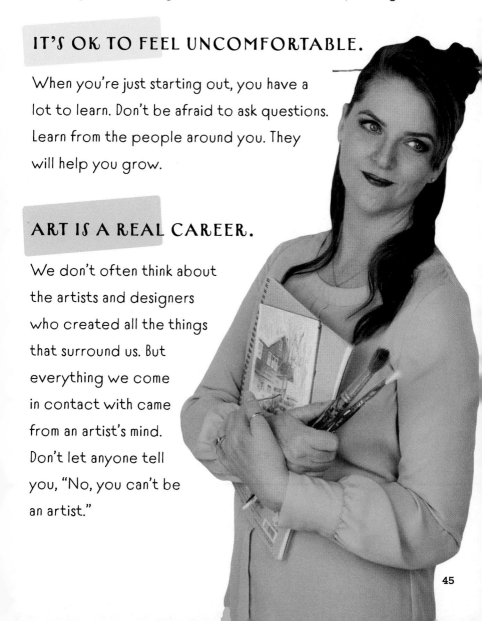

CHAPTER 5
YOU CAN BE A THEME PARK DESIGNER!

Here's a painting I did based on my travels around the world.

✒ LET'S BRAINSTORM ✒

Start imagining the theme park ride of your dreams. You can do this with some friends or by yourself. Begin by brainstorming, which is simply dreaming up and writing down ideas for the coolest ride you can think of. Here are some questions to help get you started:

What type of rides do you love the most?

Is there a place—real or imagined—that you'd love to visit?

Is there a book, movie, or TV show that could be turned into a ride?

Roller coaster

Water ride

Dark ride

Family ride

Transportation ride

Motion simulator ride

3D ride

Something else?

_____

Circle the words that best describe your ride idea.

Circle the words that best describe how riders will feel.

Happy

Excited

Scared

Surprised

Giggly

Relaxed

Energized

Thoughtful

In what kind of setting does your ride take place? What will the environment, or the space the ride vehicle moves through, look like?

Example: My ride takes place in "outer space." The ride will be built in a dark building with lots of twinkle lights and projections of planets and moons on the ceiling. Each room will have a different space city with pretend buildings and robotic characters.

What type of vehicle will your riders sit within? How does it move?

Example: My ride vehicle is a "flying space car" that will fit four people. It will have four wheels and will be driven by a robot.

Draw a picture of it here.

Describe what happens in the ride. Is there a story? Characters?

Example: Riders will travel to different space cities via a robot tour guide and flying car. They will get to see cool technology, aliens, and a meteor shower along the way.

What music and sounds will your riders hear?

Example: Riders will listen to a funny robot tour guide while interesting music plays on the space radio.

୧ BIRD'S-EYE VIEW ୧

Tracey's favorite thing to do is draw a bird's-eye view of the attraction she's designing. It's a view from above, like a map, with little peeks into what the ride or the world might look like. You can label different parts of your drawing and make notes that give more details.

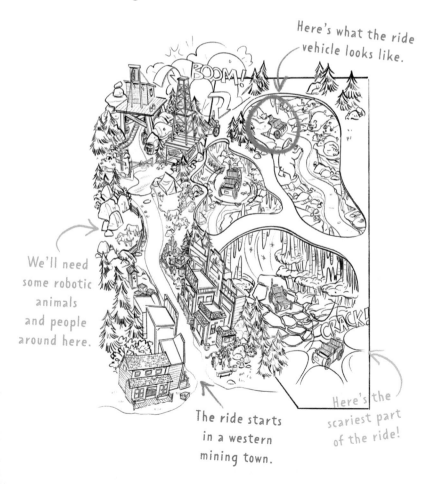

Here's what the ride vehicle looks like.

We'll need some robotic animals and people around here.

The ride starts in a western mining town.

Here's the scariest part of the ride!

Draw a bird's-eye view map of your ride on these two pages.

✍ THINK LIKE ✍ AN ARTIST

One way to practice drawing is to look at a real-life object and then try to recreate it on paper. This involves a lot of observation, which means you look at something carefully and recognize all of its details.

We're going to use a cat as an example, but you can choose any object. Follow these instructions to understand a real artist's process!

YOU WILL NEED:

- Pencil
- Eraser
- Plain paper (or flip the page to find a blank drawing page)
- An object that you'd like to learn how to draw

1. If you want to learn how to draw a cat, look at a real-life cat up close. Try to understand where the cat's joints are. Joints are where bones connect with each other. It's the parts of a body that bend, like your elbow, wrist, and knee.

2. All drawings start with a skeleton, which can just be simple lines like a stick figure with small circles to represent the joints. Knowing how an object is put together is very important!

3. Even if you're drawing a chair or a car, you'll still want to outline a simple skeleton with joints that show where the object moves or bends.

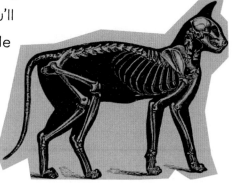

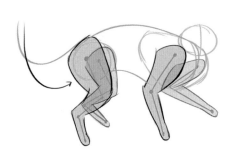

4. Next, look for basic shapes. For example, a cat's head is a circle and a cat's body is an oval. Artists start every drawing with very basic shapes—even the most complicated drawings!

5. Draw a midline. On a human or animal, it's usually the spine, which runs from the bottom of your head down the middle of your back.

6. Now you can start adding in all the details. Start layering them on top using your basic shapes and midline as a guide. Erase any lines or shapes that you don't need anymore.

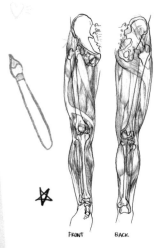

FRONT   BACK

CHAPTER 6
LOOK UP!

Here are some examples of what you might find in my sketchbook!

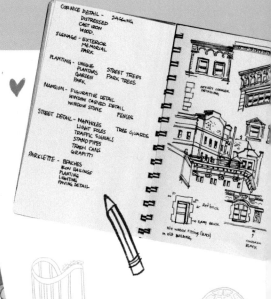

WHY WE LOOK UP TO TRACEY

SHE'S CURIOUS.

Tracey is always in awe of the world around her. She always asks questions and never stops learning new things.

SHE'S AN EXPLORER.

Tracey loves studying history and cultures. She travels to new places around the world and experiences new things.

SHE'S A PROBLEM-SOLVER.

When faced with a challenge, Tracey doesn't get discouraged. She can dream up a creative solution in no time.

SHE'S IMAGINATIVE.

As a designer, Tracey always has new ideas up her sleeve. She's not afraid to share them with others—even if those ideas end up in a drawer instead of in a theme park.

SHE'S SCIENTIFIC.

Tracey is an artist who is also very analytical—that means she thinks through things thoughtfully and carefully. She observes every detail.

Describe a time you fixed a problem with a creative solution.

List three things that always make you wonder, "How does that work?"

Talk about a time you shared your ideas with others and they loved it.

In what ways are you artistic? In what ways are you scientific?

Name a place or a time period that you'd love to explore.

Describe a challenge that you overcame.

✑ LOOK UP MORE! ✑

There's so much more to learn. If any of the topics in this book inspired you, head to the library to find more information or ask an adult to help you search online. Here are some ideas to get you started.

DRAWING

Ask an adult to search #DrawWithRob on YouTube to find fun drawing tutorials from children's book author and illustrator Rob Biddulph.

DESIGN

Check out **kidsthinkdesign.org** to learn more about the many different fields of design from fashion design to book design to interior design.

HOW THINGS WORK

Pick up a copy of *The Way Things Work Now* by David Macaulay to learn all about different kinds of machines and technologies like jumbo jets, wifi, lasers, and 3D printers.

ABOUT THE EXPERT

Tracey Noce is a design-focused Creative Director for theme parks and physically-based entertainment experiences. She leads projects with talented and diverse teams through initial creative development all the way into design and production. As an illustration and entertainment design graduate of ArtCenter College of Design, she uses a multitude of skills and more than 15 years of theme park design experience to craft exceptional environments and attractions. She constantly strives to create worlds that use design and psychology to capture people's imaginations. Visit her website at **thechubbymermaid.com.**

ABOUT THE AUTHOR

Aubre Andrus is an award-winning children's book author with dozens of books published by American Girl, National Geographic Kids, Lonely Planet Kids, Disney, Scholastic, and more. Her titles encourage kids to be kind and be curious, and she is committed to writing books that empower girls and inspire them to become the leaders of tomorrow. Aubre received her degree in journalism and film from the University of Wisconsin. She currently lives in Los Angeles with her husband and daughter. Visit her website at **aubreandrus.com**.

WHO'S NEXT?

Meet Dr. Maya, a food scientist who believes ice cream can change the world. Maya does what she loves, which is traveling the globe, developing delicious flavors, and sharing her love of science with everyone.

Meet Zi, a video game developer who was an artist before she was an engineer. Zi uses technology to transform ideas into games that entertain people around the world.

Parents and educators, visit **thelookupseries.com** to see who you can meet next and to find video interviews, free downloads, and more.

Made in United States
Orlando, FL
19 April 2022

17004082R00038